This is a Parragon Book
This edition published in 2005

Parragon
Queen Street House
4 Queen Street
Bath BA1 1HE, UK

ISBN: 1-40546-229-9

Printed in China

Produced by
THE BRIDGEWATER BOOK COMPANY LTD

Photography Ian Parsons
Home Economist Sara Hesketh

Cover Photography Calvey Taylor-Haw
Home Economist Ruth Pollock

NOTES FOR THE READER

- This book uses both metric and imperial measurements. Follow the same units of measurement throughout; do not mix metric and imperial.

- All spoon measurements are level: teaspoons are assumed to be 5 ml, and tablespoons are assumed to be 15 ml.

- Unless otherwise stated, milk is assumed to be full fat, eggs and individual vegetables such as potatoes are medium, and pepper is freshly ground black pepper.

- Recipes using raw or very lightly cooked eggs should be avoided by infants, the elderly, pregnant women, convalescents, and anyone suffering from an illness.

- Optional ingredients, variations or serving suggestions have not been included in the calculations.

- The times given are an approximate guide only. Preparation times differ according to the techniques used by different people and the cooking times may also vary.

contents

introduction

One-pot meals are the perfect solution for today's busy cooks. Whether it be a fortifying main-meal soup, an aromatic stew or casserole, or a hearty bake or gratin, a one-pot meal will look after itself while you do other things. They may not be fashionable food, but these are unpretentious, soul-satisfying dishes. They are also flexible as to timing, and can easily be kept waiting for late-comers. And in most recipes leftovers can be reheated, to taste even better next time around.

Each of these dishes is a self-contained meal – perhaps needing just a simple salad and a hunk of bread. Because the food is cooked and served in a single pot, you will not be confronted with a pile of dirty dishes either.

To cook on top of the stove, you will need a medium-to-large saucepan with a heavy flat base which prevents the contents from sticking and burning.

Hungarian beef goulash
page 16

chicken, beans & spinach with olives
page 40

Depending on the recipe, stove-top meals can also be prepared in a heavy-based, high-sided frying pan or sauté pan.

For dishes that are started on top of the stove and finished in the oven, use a sturdy flameproof casserole or braising pan with ovenproof handles. All pans should have a well-fitting lid to keep the steam in and concentrate the flavours.

easy

Recipes are graded as follows:
1 spoon = easy;
2 spoons = very easy;
3 spoons = extremely easy.

serves 4

Recipes generally serve four people. Simply halve the ingredients to serve two, taking care not to mix metric and imperial measurements.

15 minutes

Preparation time. Where marinating or soaking are involved, these times have been added on separately: eg, 15 minutes + 30 minutes to marinate.

40 minutes

Cooking time. Cooking times do not include the cooking of side dishes or accompaniments served with the main dishes.

baked mediterranean vegetables with feta
page 74

seafood hotpot with red wine & tomatoes
page 94

Thick, hearty soups such as Scotch Broth provide a nourishing meal-in-a-bowl, while the rich mellow flavours of traditional stews, such as Hungarian Beef Goulash or Beef Bourguignon, will satisfy the most voracious of appetites. Chilli-lovers will enjoy Speedy Chilli Beef, as well as the robust spicy flavours of pork and beef in Mexican Meat Stew. There are also recipes for comforting casseroles and bakes with crisp toppings of garlicky breadcrumbs or bubbling cheese – perfect for a winter supper or weekend lunch.

meat one-pots

winter minestrone with sausage

easy serves 4

30 minutes 40 minutes

ingredients

3 tbsp olive oil

250 g/9 oz coarse-textured pork sausage,
  peeled and cut into chunks

1 onion, sliced thinly

2 garlic cloves, chopped very finely

200 g/7 oz canned chopped tomatoes

2 tbsp chopped fresh mixed herbs, such as
  flat-leaved parsley, sage and marjoram

1 celery stick, sliced thinly

1 carrot, diced

1 small red pepper, deseeded and diced

850 ml/1½ pints chicken stock

salt and pepper

50 g/1¾ oz short macaroni

75 g/2¾ oz canned, drained haricot beans

115 g/4 oz frozen peas

2 tbsp freshly grated Parmesan cheese, plus
  extra to serve

4 thick slices ciabatta or French bread,
  to serve

Heat the oil in a large saucepan over a medium–low heat. Add the sausage and onion. Cook, stirring occasionally, until the onion is just coloured.

Add the garlic, tomatoes and herbs. Cook for 5 minutes, stirring. Add the celery, carrot and pepper, cover and cook for 5 minutes.

Pour in the stock. Bring to the boil, then cover and simmer gently for 30 minutes.

Season with salt and pepper. Add the macaroni and beans and simmer for about 15 minutes, or until the macaroni is just tender.

Stir in the peas and cook for 5 minutes more. Stir in the 2 tablespoons of Parmesan.

To serve, place the bread in individual serving bowls. Ladle the soup over the bread and leave to stand for a few minutes. Serve with plenty of freshly grated Parmesan.

ham and root soup

easy   serves 4

20 minutes   1 hour

ingredients

2 tbsp vegetable oil
1 fresh bay leaf, shredded
1 tsp finely chopped fresh rosemary
200 g/7 oz piece of ham, diced
1 large onion, chopped finely
2 celery sticks, diced

800 g/1 lb 12 oz peeled root vegetables,
  diced
1 litre/1¾ pints chicken or ham stock
salt and pepper

chopped fresh chives, to garnish

Heat the oil with the bay leaf and rosemary in a large saucepan over a medium heat. Add the ham and stir-fry for a few minutes, or until beginning to crisp around the edges. Remove with a perforated spoon and set aside.

Add the onion, celery and root vegetables to the pan. Stir well, then cover and cook over a medium–low heat for 15 minutes.

Pour in the stock. Bring to the boil, then simmer, partially covered, for 30 minutes.

Purée about half the mixture in a blender or food processor, leaving the rest in the pan. Pour the purée back into the saucepan. Stir in the ham and cook over a medium–low heat until heated through.

Season with salt, bearing in mind the saltiness of the ham, and freshly ground black pepper. Sprinkle with chives and serve.

scotch broth

very easy   serves 6

30 minutes   2 hours
15 minutes

ingredients

1 large onion, quartered

6 lamb shanks, weighing about
   1.6 kg/3 lb 8 oz

1 head of garlic, unpeeled, the outer loose
   layers removed

1 tbsp vegetable oil

4 rashers unsmoked bacon, diced

1 large onion, diced

3 carrots, sliced

1 small swede, cut into chunks

1 small celeriac, cut into chunks

3 leeks, halved lengthways and sliced
   thickly

3 sprigs fresh thyme

1 fresh bay leaf

1 tsp salt

1 tsp pepper

850 ml/1½ pints chicken or beef stock

55 g/2 oz pearl barley

4 tbsp chopped fresh parsley

Heat the oven to 230°C/450°F/Gas Mark 8. Roast the quartered onion, lamb and garlic in a roasting tin for 30 minutes, or until well browned, turning occasionally. Turn into a large heavy saucepan. Pour over water to cover. Slowly bring to the boil, skimming off any foam. Cook over a low heat, partially covered, for 1¼ hours.

Crisp the bacon in the oil in a large saucepan. Add the onion, vegetables, herbs and seasoning. Pour on the the stock and add the barley. Bring to the boil, then simmer 35–40 minutes.

Remove the lamb and garlic from the first pan with a perforated spoon. Strip the meat from the bones and squeeze out the garlic pulp. Line a sieve with kitchen paper. Strain the lamb cooking liquid into a bowl. Blot up any surface fat with kitchen paper. Add 700 ml/1¼ pints of the strained liquid, with the meat and garlic pulp, to the vegetables in the saucepan. Bring to the boil, then simmer for 10 minutes. Stir in the parsley just before serving.

mexican meat stew

extremely easy   serves 4

30 minutes   3 hours

ingredients

3 tbsp vegetable oil
450 g/1 lb stewing beef, cubed
450 g/1 lb boneless pork, cubed
1 onion, chopped finely
1 red pepper, deseeded and chopped
2–4 green chillies, deseeded and
　chopped finely
2 garlic cloves, chopped very finely
1.2 kg/2 lb 10 oz canned chopped tomatoes
3 tbsp lemon juice

125 ml/4 fl oz beef stock
4 tbsp chopped fresh parsley
1 tsp ground cumin
½ tsp dried oregano
½ tsp sugar
salt and pepper

3 tbsp chopped fresh coriander, to garnish

plain boiled rice, to serve

Heat the oil in a large flameproof casserole over a medium–high heat. Add the meat in batches and cook until browned on all sides. Remove each batch with a perforated spoon, transfer to a bowl and set aside.

Add the onion and pepper, and cook for 5 minutes, or until soft. Add the chillies and garlic, and cook until the garlic is just coloured. Return the meat and any juices to the casserole.

Add all the remaining ingredients, except the coriander. Bring to the boil, stirring. Cover and simmer over a low heat for 2 hours, stirring occasionally.

Remove the lid and simmer for 30–40 minutes, or until the sauce has thickened and the meat is very tender. Add more salt if necessary.

Garnish with the coriander just before serving. Serve with rice.

hungarian beef goulash

extremely
easy

serves 4

30 minutes

3 hours

ingredients

2 tbsp vegetable oil

675 g/1 lb 8 oz stewing beef, cubed

3 onions, chopped finely

1 green pepper, deseeded and diced

2 garlic cloves, chopped very finely

2 tbsp tomato purée

2 tbsp plain flour

400 g/14 oz canned chopped tomatoes

250 ml/9 fl oz beef stock

1 fresh bay leaf

3 tbsp chopped fresh parsley

1 tbsp paprika

1 tsp salt

¼ tsp pepper

TO SERVE

buttered noodles

soured cream

Heat the oil in a flameproof casserole over a medium–high heat. Add the meat and fry until evenly browned. Remove with a perforated spoon, transfer to a bowl and set aside.

Add the onions and pepper. Cook for 5 minutes, stirring occasionally, until soft. Add the garlic and cook until just coloured. Stir in the tomato purée and flour. Cook for 1 minute, stirring continuously.

Return the meat to the pan. Add the remaining ingredients and bring to the boil. Cover and simmer over a low heat for 2½ hours, stirring occasionally. Add water or more stock if necessary.

Remove the lid and simmer for 15 minutes, stirring to prevent sticking, until the sauce has thickened and the meat is very tender.

Serve with buttered noodles and a bowl of soured cream.

beef bourguignon

very easy   serves 6

40 minutes   3 hours 15 minutes

ingredients

2 tbsp olive oil

175 g/6 oz piece unsmoked bacon, sliced
  into thin strips

1.3 kg/3 lb stewing beef, cut into 5-cm/
  2-inch pieces

2 carrots, sliced

2 onions, chopped

2 garlic cloves, chopped very finely

3 tbsp plain flour

700 ml/1¼ pints red wine

350–450 ml/12–16 fl oz beef stock

bouquet garni sachet

1 tsp salt

¼ tsp pepper

3 tbsp butter

350 g/12 oz pickling onions

350 g/12 oz button mushrooms

2 tbsp chopped fresh parsley, to garnish

Lightly brown the bacon in the oil in a large casserole (2–3 minutes). Remove
with a perforated spoon. Brown the beef in batches, drain and keep with the bacon.
Soften the carrots and chopped onions in the same pan for 5 minutes. Add the
garlic and fry until just coloured. Return the meat and bacon to the pan. Sprinkle
on the flour and cook for 1 minute, stirring. Add the wine and enough stock to
cover, the bouquet garni, salt and pepper. Bring to the boil, cover and simmer
gently for 3 hours.

Cook the pickling onions till soft in a covered frying pan in half the butter.
Remove with a perforated spoon and keep warm. Fry the mushrooms in the
remaining butter. Remove and keep warm.

Sieve the casserole liquid into a saucepan. Wipe the casserole and tip in the meat,
bacon, mushrooms and onions. Remove the surface fat from the cooking liquid,
simmer for 1–2 minutes to reduce, then pour over the meat and vegetables. Serve
sprinkled with parsley.

sausage & tomato hotpot

easy   serves 4

20 minutes   1 hour

ingredients

2 tbsp olive oil

225 g/8 oz coarse-textured pure pork
   sausage, peeled and cut into chunks

2 onions, chopped finely

4 carrots, sliced thickly

6 potatoes, cut into chunks

2 large garlic cloves, chopped very finely

2 tsp chopped fresh rosemary

2 tsp chopped fresh thyme or oregano

1.2 kg/2 lb 10 oz canned chopped tomatoes

salt and pepper

2 tbsp chopped fresh flat-leaved parsley,
   to garnish

Heat the oil in a large heavy-based saucepan over a medium–high heat. Add the sausage and fry until browned. Remove from the pan with a perforated spoon and set aside.

Reduce the heat to medium. Add the onions, carrots, potatoes, garlic, rosemary and thyme to the pan. Cover and cook gently for 10 minutes, stirring occasionally.

Return the sausage to the pan. Pour in the tomatoes and bring to the boil. Season with salt and pepper. Cover and simmer over a medium–low heat, stirring occasionally, for 45 minutes until the vegetables are tender.

Sprinkle with the parsley just before serving.

beef pot roast with potatoes & dill

very easy   serves 6

40 minutes   3 hours
30 minutes

ingredients

2½ tbsp plain flour
1 tsp salt
¼ tsp pepper
1.6 kg/3 lb 8 oz rolled brisket
2 tbsp vegetable oil
2 tbsp butter
1 onion, chopped finely
2 celery sticks, diced
2 carrots, diced

1 tsp dill seed
1 tsp dried thyme or oregano
350 ml/12 fl oz red wine
150–225 ml/9 fl oz beef stock
4 or 5 potatoes, cut into large chunks and
   boiled till just tender

2 tbsp fresh dill, to garnish

Mix 2 tablespoons of flour with the salt and pepper in a shallow dish. Dip the meat to coat. Heat the oil in a casserole and brown the meat all over. Transfer to a plate. Add 1 tablespoon of butter to the casserole and cook the onion, celery, carrots, dill seed and thyme for 5 minutes. Replace the meat and juices in the pan.

Pour in the wine and enough stock to reach one-third of the way up the meat. Bring to the boil, cover and cook for 3 hours in a preheated oven at 140°C/275°F/ Gas Mark 1, turning every half hour. After 2 hours, add the potatoes and more stock if needed.

When ready, transfer the meat and vegetables to a warm serving dish. Sieve the cooking liquid into a saucepan.

Mix the remaining butter and flour to a paste. Bring the cooking liquid to the boil. Whisk in small pieces of the flour/butter paste, whisking until the sauce is smooth. Pour the sauce over the meat and vegetables. Sprinkle with the dill and serve.

speedy chilli beef

extremely easy   serves 4

15 minutes   45 minutes

ingredients

3 tbsp vegetable oil
450 g/1 lb minced beef
1 onion, chopped finely
1 green pepper, deseeded and diced
2 garlic cloves, chopped very finely
800 g/1 lb 12 oz canned chopped tomatoes
400g/14 oz canned red kidney beans,
    drained and rinsed

1 tsp ground cumin
1 tsp salt
1 tsp sugar
1–3 tsp chilli powder
2 tbsp chopped fresh coriander

Heat the oil in a large flameproof casserole over a medium–high heat. Add the beef and cook, stirring, until lightly browned.

Reduce the heat to medium. Add the onion, pepper and garlic. Cook for 5 minutes, or until soft.

Stir in the remaining ingredients, except coriander. Bring to the boil. Simmer over a medium–low heat, stirring frequently, for 30 minutes.

Stir in the coriander just before serving.

beef, mushroom & rice casserole

extremely easy   serves 4

15 minutes   35 minutes

ingredients

3 tbsp olive oil
400 g/14 oz minced beef
1 onion, chopped finely
1 pepper, deseeded and chopped finely
150 g/5½ oz mushrooms, sliced

2 tbsp tomato purée
250 g/9 oz long-grain rice
600 ml/1 pint hot beef stock
salt and pepper
75 g/2¾ oz freshly grated Cheddar cheese

Heat the oil in a high-sided lidded casserole over a medium–high heat. Add the beef and cook, stirring, until lightly browned.

Reduce the heat to medium. Add the onion, pepper, mushrooms and tomato purée. Cook for 5 minutes, or until soft.

Stir in the rice. Cook gently, stirring, for 3–4 minutes.

Pour in the hot stock. Season with salt and pepper. Bring to the boil. Cover tightly and simmer over a low heat for about 20 minutes, or until the rice is tender and has absorbed most of the liquid.

Sprinkle with the cheese. Cover and leave to stand while the cheese melts. Serve at once, straight from the dish.

spanish ham & rice one-pot

very easy   serves 4

15 minutes   35 minutes

ingredients

2 tbsp olive oil

1 onion, chopped finely

1 red pepper, deseeded and chopped finely

350 g/12 oz piece of ham, cubed

2 tsp paprika

400 g/14 oz canned chopped tomatoes

200 g/7 oz long-grain rice

450 ml/16 fl oz hot chicken stock

salt and pepper

85 g/3 oz frozen peas

Heat the oil in a large heavy-based saucepan over a medium heat. Add the onion and pepper. Cook for 5 minutes, or until soft.

Stir in the ham, paprika, tomatoes and rice. Cook, stirring continuously, for 3–4 minutes.

Pour in the hot stock. Season with salt and pepper. Bring to the boil. Cover tightly and simmer over a low heat for 15 minutes.

Add the peas. Cover and cook for another 5 minutes, or until the rice is tender and has absorbed most of the liquid.

Remove the pan from the heat and leave the dish to stand for 5 minutes before serving.

lamb, garlic & bean casserole

very easy   serves 4

45 minutes   2 hours
             30 minutes

ingredients

2 tbsp olive oil, plus extra for drizzling
900 g/2 lb boneless lamb, cut into
   4-cm/1½-inch cubes
2 onions, chopped finely
1 tbsp chopped fresh rosemary
12 large garlic cloves, peeled and left whole
2 or 3 anchovy fillets, chopped roughly
2 tbsp plain flour
½ tsp pepper

600 ml/1 pint chicken or lamb stock
225 g/8 oz dried cannellini or haricot
   beans, soaked overnight and drained
salt, to taste
115 g/4 oz stale, coarse breadcrumbs

chopped fresh flat-leaved parsley,
   to garnish

Heat 1 tablespoon of the oil in a flameproof casserole. When very hot, cook the lamb in batches until evenly browned. Transfer to a plate. Cook the onion and rosemary in the remaining oil in the casserole for 5–7 minutes, stirring, until golden brown. Reduce the heat, stir in the garlic and anchovies, and cook for 1 minute.

Preheat the oven to 150°C/300°F/Gas Mark 2. Return the meat and any juices to the casserole. Sprinkle with the flour and stir well. Season with the pepper. Pour in the stock, stirring continuously. Add the drained beans.

Bring to the boil, cover tightly and cook in the preheated oven for 2 hours, or until soft. Remove from the oven. Season with salt.

Spread the breadcrumbs over the lamb and beans. Drizzle a little olive oil over the top. Place under a preheated grill for a few minutes until the crumbs are golden brown. Sprinkle with parsley and serve immediately.

Versatile poultry forms the basis of a wealth of one-pot meals. Chicken features widely in appetising main-meal soups, spicy stews and hotpots, and easily prepared bean and rice dishes. To get the taste buds tingling, try Spicy Chicken Hotpot or New Orleans-style Chicken Jambalaya. Sweet and meaty duck goes oriental in a richly flavoured stew of shiitake mushrooms and water chestnuts. Turkey is the main ingredient in what must be the speediest one-pot meal of all – a stir-fry of vibrant green mangetouts and pak choi.

poultry one-pots

chicken, squash & spinach soup

easy   serves 4

20 minutes   1 hour

ingredients

1 tbsp olive oil

1 tbsp butter

3 boneless, skinless chicken breasts, cubed

2 small leeks, green part included,
  sliced thinly

1 small butternut squash, cut into
  2-cm/¾-inch cubes

1 small green chilli (optional), deseeded
  and chopped very finely

400 g/14 oz canned chickpeas, drained
  and rinsed

¼ tsp ground cumin

salt and pepper

1 litre/1¾ pints chicken stock

115 g/4 oz baby spinach, chopped coarsely

warm crusty bread, to serve

Heat the oil and butter in a large saucepan over a medium–low heat. Add the chicken, leeks, squash and chilli, if using. Cover and cook for 10 minutes, stirring occasionally, until the vegetables are beginning to soften.

Add the chickpeas, cumin, salt and pepper.

Pour in the stock. Bring to the boil, then simmer over a low heat for 40 minutes, or until the squash is tender.

Stir in the spinach. Cook for a few more minutes until the spinach is just wilted, and serve with warm, crusty bread while piping hot.

chicken, sausage & bean stew

easy   serves 4

35 minutes   45 minutes

ingredients

2 tbsp vegetable oil

4 boneless, skinless chicken breasts, cubed

225 g/8 oz coarse-textured pork sausage,
   cut into large chunks

4 frankfurter sausages, halved

1 onion, chopped finely

3 carrots, sliced finely

1 garlic clove, chopped very finely

1 tsp dried thyme

¼–½ tsp dried chilli flakes

400 g/14 oz canned chopped tomatoes

400 g/14 oz canned cannellini beans,
   drained and rinsed

150 ml/5 fl oz chicken stock

salt and pepper

chopped fresh flat-leaved parsley,
   to garnish

Heat the oil in a large, heavy-based saucepan over a medium–high heat. Cook the chicken, pork sausage and frankfurters until lightly browned. Reduce the heat to medium. Add the onion and carrots. Cook for 5 minutes, or until soft.

Stir in the garlic, thyme and chilli flakes. Cook for 1 minute. Add the tomatoes, beans and chicken stock. Season with salt and pepper. Bring to the boil, then simmer over a low heat for 20–30 minutes, stirring occasionally.

Garnish with parsley just before serving.

spicy chicken hotpot

very easy   serves 4

45 minutes   1 hour
              15 minutes

ingredients

2 tbsp vegetable oil

600 g/1 lb 5 oz skinless, boneless chicken
  breasts, cubed

1 tsp cumin seeds, crushed

2 tsp coriander seeds, crushed

2 tsp dried oregano or thyme

1 onion, chopped

2 potatoes, cubed

2 sweet potatoes, cubed

3 carrots, sliced thickly

3 garlic cloves, chopped very finely

1 or 2 red chillies, deseeded and
  chopped finely

1 tsp salt

¼ tsp pepper

400 g/14 oz canned chopped tomatoes

450 ml/16 fl oz chicken stock

175 g/6 oz green beans, cut into
  4-cm/1½-inch pieces

8 x frozen sweetcorn cob quarters

chopped fresh coriander, to garnish

Heat the oil in a casserole over a medium–high heat. Cook the chicken until lightly browned, stirring frequently. Stir in the cumin, coriander and oregano. Cook for 1 minute.

Reduce the heat to medium. Add the onion, potatoes, sweet potatoes, carrots, garlic and chillies. Cover and cook for 10 minutes, stirring occasionally, until beginning to soften.

Add the salt and pepper. Pour in the tomatoes and stock. Bring to the boil, cover and simmer over a medium–low heat for 30 minutes.

Add the beans and sweetcorn. Cook for 15 minutes more, or until the beans are just tender.

Garnish with coriander just before serving.

chicken, beans & spinach with olives

very easy   serves 4

20 minutes   45 minutes

ingredients

2 tbsp olive oil

600 g/1 lb 5 oz skinless, boneless chicken
    breasts, cut into chunks

1 small onion, chopped finely

2 celery sticks, diced

3 large garlic cloves, chopped finely

2 tsp chopped fresh rosemary

¼ tsp dried chilli flakes

400 g/14 oz canned chopped tomatoes

400 g/14 oz canned cannellini beans,
    drained and rinsed

250 ml/9 fl oz chicken stock

salt and pepper

350 g/12 oz baby spinach, chopped roughly

8–10 stoned black olives (sliced),
    to garnish

Heat the oil in a casserole over a medium–high heat. Cook the chicken until
lightly browned, stirring frequently.

Reduce the heat to medium. Add the onion and celery. Cook for 5 minutes,
or until soft.

Stir in the garlic, rosemary and chilli flakes. Cook for another minute. Add the
tomatoes, beans and chicken stock. Season with salt and pepper.

Bring to the boil, then simmer over a medium–low heat for 20 minutes. Stir in
the spinach. Cook for about 3 minutes, or until wilted.

Garnish with the olives and serve immediately.

chicken with rice, mushrooms & tomatoes

very easy   serves 4

15 minutes   1 hour

ingredients

2 tbsp olive oil
650 g/1 lb 7 oz boneless, skinless chicken
   breasts, cubed
1 onion, chopped finely
115 g/4 oz mushrooms, sliced finely
2 garlic cloves, chopped very finely

4 tbsp chopped fresh flat-leaved parsley
350 g/12 oz long-grain rice
400 g/14 oz canned chopped tomatoes
salt and pepper
450 ml/16 fl oz hot chicken stock

Heat the oil in a large heavy-based frying pan over a medium–high heat. Cook the chicken until lightly browned, stirring frequently.

Reduce the heat to medium. Add the onion and mushrooms. Cook for 5 minutes, or until soft. Stir in the garlic and 2 tablespoons of the parsley. Cook for 1 minute.

Add the rice and cook for 5 minutes, stirring constantly. Add the tomatoes. Season with salt and pepper. Cook for another minute. Stir in the hot stock. Bring to the boil, then cover tightly and simmer over a low heat for 20–25 minutes, or until the rice is tender.

Remove from the heat and leave the dish to stand, covered, for 10 minutes before serving. Sprinkle with the remaining parsley to garnish and serve.

chicken jambalaya

easy · serves 4

30 minutes · 1 hour 10 minutes

ingredients

3 tbsp vegetable oil
900 g/2 lb boneless, skinless chicken
 thighs
1 onion, chopped finely
2 red or green peppers, deseeded and
 chopped finely
2 garlic cloves, chopped very finely
300 g/10½ oz long-grain rice
2 tbsp tomato purée
1 tsp dried thyme

1 tsp dried oregano
¼ tsp dried chilli flakes
225 g/8 oz chorizo sausage, cut into chunks
3 plum tomatoes, chopped roughly
salt and pepper
600 ml/1 pint hot chicken stock

3 spring onions, green part included,
 chopped finely, to garnish

Heat the oil in a flameproof casserole over a medium–high heat. Cook the chicken in batches until lightly browned, stirring frequently. Remove with a perforated spoon and transfer to a plate.

Reduce the heat to medium. Add the onion and peppers. Cook for 5 minutes, or until soft. Add the garlic and cook for 1 minute. Add the rice and cook for 5 minutes, stirring constantly.

Add the tomato purée, thyme, oregano, chilli flakes, chorizo and tomatoes. Season with salt and pepper. Cook for 2–3 minutes.

Return the chicken and any juices to the casserole. Stir in the hot stock. Bring to the boil, then cover tightly and simmer over a low heat for 20–25 minutes, or until the rice is tender.

Remove from the heat. Sprinkle with the spring onions. Cover and leave to stand for 10 minutes before serving.

braised oriental duck

very easy   serves 4

30 minutes   2 hours

ingredients

3 tbsp soy sauce
¼ tsp Chinese five-spice powder
¼ tsp pepper; pinch of salt
4 duck legs or breasts, cut into pieces
3 tbsp vegetable oil
1 tsp dark sesame oil
1 tsp finely chopped ginger root
1 large garlic clove, finely chopped
4 spring onions, white part sliced thickly, green part shredded

2 tbsp rice wine or dry sherry
1 tbsp oyster sauce
3 whole star anise
2 tsp black peppercorns
450–600 ml/16 fl oz–1 pint chicken stock or water
6 dried shiitake mushrooms, soaked in warm water for 20 minutes
225 g/8 oz canned water chestnuts, drained
2 tbsp cornflour

Combine 1 tablespoon of the soy sauce, five-spice powder, pepper and salt and rub over the duck pieces. Brown the duck pieces in 2½ tablespoons of vegetable oil, remove and transfer to a plate.

Drain the fat from the casserole and wipe out. Heat the sesame oil and remaining vegetable oil. Add the ginger and garlic. Cook for a few seconds. Add the white spring onion. Cook for a few seconds. Return the duck to the pan. Add the rice wine, oyster sauce, star anise, peppercorns and remaining soy sauce. Pour in enough stock to just cover. Bring to the boil, cover and simmer gently for 1½ hours, adding more water if necessary.

Drain the mushrooms and squeeze dry. Slice the caps and add to the duck with the water chestnuts. Simmer for 20 minutes more.

Mix the cornflour with 2 tablespoons of the cooking liquid to a smooth paste. Add to the remaining liquid, stirring until thickened. Garnish with the green spring onion shreds and serve.

turkey stir-fry with noodles

easy   serves 4

20 minutes   20 minutes

ingredients

225 g/8 oz dried egg noodles
250 g/9 oz turkey escalopes, cut into thin
   strips
1 tsp cornflour
1 tsp sugar
¼ tsp salt
3 tbsp soy sauce
3 tbsp vegetable oil
2 tbsp dark sesame oil

6–8 shiitake mushrooms, sliced finely
115 g/4 oz mangetouts, halved lengthways
225 g/8 oz pak choi, cut into 1-cm/½-inch
   diagonal slices
6 thin slices fresh ginger root, chopped
   very finely
1 large garlic clove, chopped very finely
salt and pepper

Cook the noodles according to the packet instructions. Drain, rinse with cold water and set aside.

Spread the turkey strips on a plate. Dredge with the cornflour, sugar, salt and soy sauce. Toss well to coat.

Heat 2 tablespoons of vegetable oil and 1 tablespoon of sesame oil in a wok or large frying pan over a high heat. When very hot, add the turkey. Stir-fry for 2 minutes. Add the mushrooms, mangetouts and pak choi. Stir-fry for 2 minutes. Add the ginger and garlic. Stir-fry for 1 minute. Season with salt and pepper. Transfer the turkey and vegetables to a warm dish.

Reduce the heat to medium. Add the remaining oils to the pan. When hot, add the cooked noodles. Stir-fry for 2 minutes, or until heated through and coated with oil. Return the turkey and vegetables to the pan. Mix with the noodles and serve at once.

mexican chicken, chilli & potato pot

easy   serves 4

30 minutes   35 minutes

ingredients

2 tbsp vegetable oil

450 g/1 lb boneless, skinless chicken
  breasts, cubed

1 onion, chopped finely

1 green pepper, deseeded and chopped
  finely

1 potato, diced

1 sweet potato, diced

2 garlic cloves, chopped very finely

1 or 2 fresh green chillies, deseeded and
  chopped very finely

200 g/7 oz can chopped tomatoes

½ tsp dried oregano

½ tsp salt

¼ tsp pepper

4 tbsp chopped fresh coriander

450 ml/16 fl oz chicken stock

Heat the oil in a large heavy-based saucepan over a medium–high heat. Cook the chicken until lightly browned.

Reduce the heat to medium. Add the onion, pepper, potato and sweet potato. Cover and cook for 5 minutes, stirring occasionally, until the vegetables begin to soften.

Add the garlic and chillies. Cook for 1 minute. Stir in the tomatoes, oregano, salt, pepper and 2 tablespoons of the coriander. Cook for 1 minute.

Pour in the stock. Bring to the boil, then cover and simmer over a medium–low heat for 15–20 minutes, or until the chicken is cooked through and the vegetables are tender.

Sprinkle with the remaining coriander just before serving.

paprika chicken & rice casserole

easy   serves 4

20 minutes   1 hour

ingredients

3 tbsp vegetable oil

4 part-boned chicken breasts, about
150 g/5½ oz each

1 onion, chopped finely

2 garlic cloves, chopped very finely

200 g/7 oz long-grain rice

280 g/10 oz frozen mixed vegetables

450 ml/16 fl oz hot chicken stock

2 tsp paprika

2 tsp dried thyme

salt and pepper

175 g/6 oz Cheddar or mozzarella cheese,
coarsely grated

Heat the oil in a shallow flameproof casserole a over medium–high heat. Cook the chicken in batches until lightly browned. Remove with a perforated spoon and transfer to a plate.

Reduce the heat to medium. Add the onion. Cook for 5 minutes until soft. Add the garlic and cook for 1 minute. Stir in the rice and cook for 5 minutes, stirring constantly.

Add the frozen vegetables, the hot stock, and 1 teaspoon each of the paprika and thyme. Bring to the boil, stirring until well mixed. Season with salt and pepper. Place the chicken breasts on top of the rice mixture. Sprinkle with the remaining paprika and thyme.

Cover tightly and simmer over a low heat for 20–25 minutes, or until the liquid is absorbed and the chicken cooked through.

Remove from the heat. Sprinkle with the cheese. Place under a preheated grill for 5 minutes. Serve when the cheese has melted.

turkey, leek & cheese gratin

easy   serves 4

30 minutes   40 minutes

ingredients

115 g/4 oz short macaroni
1 small egg, beaten lightly
2 tbsp butter
4 small leeks, green part included, sliced
  finely
2 carrots, diced
1 tbsp plain flour

¼ tsp freshly grated nutmeg
250 ml/9 fl oz chicken stock
225 g/8 oz diced cooked turkey or chicken
55 g/2 oz diced ham
3 tbsp chopped fresh flat-leaved parsley
salt and pepper
100 g/3½ oz freshly grated Gruyère cheese

Cook the macaroni in plenty of boiling salted water until just tender. Drain and return to the pan. Stir in the egg and a knob of the butter, mixing well. Set aside.

Preheat the oven to 180°C/350°F/Gas Mark 4.

Melt the remaining butter in a saucepan over a medium heat. Add the leeks and carrots. Cover and cook for 5 minutes, shaking the pan occasionally, until just tender.

Add the flour and nutmeg. Cook for 1 minute, stirring constantly. Pour in the stock. Bring to the boil, stirring constantly. Stir in the turkey, ham and parsley. Season with salt and pepper.

Spread half the turkey mixture over the base of a shallow baking dish. Spread the macaroni over the turkey. Top with the remaining turkey mixture. Sprinkle with the cheese.

Bake in the preheated oven for 15–20 minutes. Serve when the cheese is golden and bubbling.

Vibrant vegetables combine with the earthy flavours of pulses, grains and pasta in deeply satisfying and nutritious one-pot meals. All are simple to prepare and make exciting eating whatever the occasion – midweek suppers or entertaining friends. Try Barley and Pepper Pilaf, or the colourful and crisp-textured Lentil and Rice Pilaf with Celery, Carrots and Orange – perfect for a festive vegetarian meal. Or experience the earthy, complex flavours of mushrooms and aubergines in Baked Mediterranean Vegetables with Feta.

vegetable
one-pots

hearty lentil & vegetable soup

very easy   serves 4

15 minutes   40 minutes

ingredients

2 tbsp vegetable oil

3 leeks, green part included, sliced finely

3 carrots, diced

2 celery sticks, quartered lengthways and
  diced

115 g/4 oz brown or green lentils

75 g/2¾ oz long-grain rice

1 litre/1¾ pints chicken stock

8 x sweetcorn cob quarters

salt and pepper

4 tbsp chopped fresh chives

soured cream, to serve

Heat the oil in a large saucepan over a medium heat. Add the leeks, carrots and celery. Cover and cook for 5–7 minutes, or until just tender. Stir in the lentils and rice.

Pour in the stock. Bring to the boil, then cover and simmer over a medium–low heat for 20 minutes.

Add the sweetcorn. Simmer for 10 minutes more, or until the lentils and rice are tender.

Season with salt and pepper. Stir in the chives. Ladle into individual bowls, top with a spoonful of soured cream and serve immediately.

beans & greens soup

very easy   serves 4

30 minutes   20 minutes

ingredients

3 tsbp olive oil

1 large white onion, sliced thinly

3 garlic cloves, chopped very finely

2 or 3 mild green chillies, such as Anaheim, deseeded and chopped

1 tsp dried oregano

250 g/9 oz shredded savoy cabbage or kale

400 g/14 oz canned borlotti beans, drained and rinsed

850 ml/1½ pints chicken or vegetable stock

salt and pepper

3 tbsp chopped fresh coriander, to garnish

Heat the oil in a large saucepan over a medium heat. Cook the onion for 5–7 minutes or until soft.

Add the garlic, chillies and oregano. Cook for a few seconds, or until the garlic is just beginning to colour. Add the cabbage, beans and stock. Season with salt and pepper.

Bring to the boil, then cover and simmmer for 7–10 minutes or until the cabbage is just tender.

Sprinkle with the coriander just before serving.

creamy potato, onion & cheese soup

very easy   serves 4

15 minutes   30 minutes

ingredients

3 tbsp butter
1 small onion, chopped finely
6 spring onions, green part included,
   chopped finely
4 potatoes, cut into chunks
700 ml/1¼ pints chicken stock
salt and pepper

150 ml/5 fl oz milk
150 ml/5 fl oz whipping cream
3 tbsp chopped fresh parsley
75 g/2¾ oz coarsely grated Cheddar cheese

fried garlic croûtons (optional), to serve

Heat the butter in a large saucepan over a medium heat. Add the onion, spring onions and potatoes. Cover and cook for 5–7 minutes until the onions are just tender.

Add the stock. Bring to the boil, then cover and simmer over a medium–low heat for 15–20 minutes, or until the potatoes are tender. Remove from the heat.

Mash the potatoes. Season with salt and pepper. Stir in the milk, cream and 2 tablespoons of the parsley. Reheat gently. Ladle into bowls. Sprinkle with the cheese and remaining parsley.

Serve with the croûtons, if using.

tomato, mushroom & macaroni hotpot

easy · serves 4

20 minutes · 30 minutes

ingredients

3 tbsp olive oil
1 onion, sliced
75 g/2¾ oz mushrooms, sliced thinly
2 garlic cloves, chopped very finely
1 tsp dried oregano
2 tbsp tomato purée
3 tbsp chopped fresh flat-leaved parsley

800 g/1lb 12 oz canned chopped tomatoes
450 ml/16 fl oz chicken stock
225 g/8 oz dried short macaroni
1 tsp salt
¼ tsp pepper

freshly grated Parmesan cheese, to serve

Heat the olive oil in a large saucepan or high-sided frying pan with a lid, over a medium heat. Add the onion and mushrooms. Cook, stirring for 5–7 minutes, or until soft.

Stir in the garlic, oregano, tomato purée and 1½ tablespoons of the parsley. Cook for 1 minute. Pour in the tomatoes and stock. Bring to the boil.

Add the macaroni, salt and pepper. Bring back to the boil. Cover and simmer over a medium–low heat for 20 minutes, stirring occasionally, or until the macaroni is tender.

Sprinkle with the remaining parsley just before serving. Serve with freshly grated Parmesan cheese.

mexican three-bean chilli hotpot

very easy   serves 6

30 minutes   2 hours

ingredients

140 g/5 oz each black beans, cannellini
  beans and pinto beans, soaked overnight
  in separate bowls
2 tbsp olive oil
1 large onion, chopped finely
2 red peppers, deseeded and diced
2 garlic cloves, chopped very finely
½ tsp cumin seeds, crushed
1 tsp coriander seeds, crushed

1 tsp dried oregano
½–2 tsp chilli powder
3 tbsp tomato purée
800 g/1 lb 12 oz canned chopped tomatoes
1 tsp sugar
1 tsp salt
600 ml/1 pint chicken or vegetable stock
3 tbsp chopped fresh coriander

Drain the beans, put in separate saucepans and cover with fresh water. Boil rapidly
for 10–15 minutes, then simmer for 35–45 minutes, or until just tender. Drain and
set aside.

Heat the oil in a large heavy-based saucepan over a medium heat. Cook the onion
and peppers for 5 minutes, or until soft.

Stir in the garlic, cumin and coriander seeds, and oregano. Cook for a few
seconds, or until the garlic is just beginning to colour. Add the chilli powder and
tomato purée. Cook for 1 minute. Add the tomatoes, sugar, salt, beans and stock.
Stir well and bring to the boil. Cover and simmer over a low heat for 45 minutes,
stirring occasionally to prevent sticking.

Stir in the coriander and remove from the heat. Ladle into individual bowls
to serve.

barley & pepper pilaf

easy   serves 4

25 minutes 1 hour
15 minutes

ingredients

1 tbsp vegetable oil
2 tbsp butter
1 onion, chopped finely
1 red pepper, deseeded and chopped finely
1 green pepper, deseeded and chopped
  finely
225 g/8 oz mushrooms, sliced thinly

2 tbsp chopped fresh flat-leaved parsley
2 garlic cloves, chopped very finely
125 g/4½ oz pearl barley
400–600 ml/14 fl oz–1 pint chicken or
  vegetable stock
salt and pepper

Heat the oil and butter in a high-sided frying pan with a lid over a medium heat. Add the onion, peppers and mushrooms. Cook for 5–7 minutes, or until soft, stirring often.

Add the parsley and garlic. Cook for 1 minute. Add the barley and mix well. Pour in 400 ml/14 fl oz of the stock. Season with salt and pepper.

Stir, bring to the boil, then cover and simmer over a low heat for about 1 hour, or until the barley is tender and most of the liquid has been absorbed. Add more stock if necessary.

Remove from the heat and leave to stand for 5 minutes. Fluff with a fork before serving.

lentil & rice pilaf with celery, carrots & orange

very easy   serves 4

30 minutes   15 minutes

ingredients

4 tbsp vegetable oil

1 red onion, chopped finely

2 tender celery sticks, leaves included, quartered lengthways and diced

2 carrots, grated coarsely

1 green chilli, deseeded and chopped finely

3 spring onions, green part included, chopped finely

40 g/1½ oz whole almonds, sliced lengthways

350 g/12 oz cooked brown basmati rice

150 g/5½ oz cooked orange lentils

175 ml/6 fl oz chicken or vegetable stock

5 tbsp fresh orange juice

salt and pepper

Heat 2 tablespoons of the oil in a high-sided frying pan with a lid over a medium heat. Add the onion. Cook for 5 minutes, or until soft.

Add the celery, carrots, chilli, spring onions and almonds. Stir-fry for 2 minutes, or until the vegetables are al dente but still brightly coloured. Transfer to a bowl and set aside.

Add the remaining oil to the pan. Stir in the rice and lentils. Cook over a medium–high heat, stirring, for 1–2 minutes, or until heated through. Reduce the heat. Stir in the stock and orange juice. Season with salt and pepper.

Return the vegetables to the pan. Toss with the rice for a few minutes until heated through. Transfer to a warm dish to serve.

chickpea & potato curry

easy   serves 6

40 minutes   2 hours

ingredients

225 g/8 oz chickpeas, soaked
3 tbsp vegetable oil
½ tsp cumin seeds
½ tsp mustard seeds
1 onion, chopped finely
2 garlic cloves, chopped very finely
2-cm/¾-inch piece fresh ginger root,
    chopped very finely
1 tsp salt
2 tsp ground coriander
1 tsp turmeric

½ tsp cayenne
2 tbsp tomato purée
400 g/14 oz canned chopped tomatoes
2 potatoes, cubed
3 tbsp chopped fresh coriander
1 tbsp lemon juice
250–300 ml/9–10 fl oz chicken or
    vegetable stock

thinly sliced white or red onion rings,
    and cooked rice, to serve

Boil the chickpeas rapidly in plenty of water for 15 minutes. Reduce the heat and boil gently for 1 hour, or until tender. Drain and set aside.

Heat the oil in a large saucepan or high-sided frying pan. Stirring all the time, add the cumin and mustard seeds, cover and cook for a few seconds, or until the seeds pop. Add the onion. Cover and cook for 3–5 minutes, or until just brown. Add the garlic and ginger. Cook for a few seconds. Stir in salt, ground coriander, turmeric and cayenne, then the tomato purée and tomatoes. Simmer for a few minutes. Add the chickpeas, potatoes and 2 tablespoons of the fresh coriander.

Stir in the lemon juice and 250 ml/9 fl oz of the stock. Bring to the boil, then simmer for 30–40 minutes, or until the potatoes are cooked. Add stock if the mixture becomes too dry.

Garnish with onion rings and the remaining coriander and serve with rice.

baked mediterranean vegetables with feta

ingredients

very easy   serves 4

40 minutes   40 minutes

1 red onion, sliced into thick rings

1 small aubergine, sliced thickly

2 large mushrooms, halved

3 red peppers, halved, cored and deseeded

3 tbsp olive oil, plus extra for brushing

3 plum tomatoes, peeled and diced

salt and pepper

2 garlic cloves, chopped very finely

1 tbsp chopped fresh flat-leaved parsley

1 tsp chopped fresh rosemary

1 tsp dried thyme or oregano

finely grated zest of 1 lemon

75 g/2¾ oz stale, coarse breadcrumbs

6–8 black olives, stoned and sliced

25 g/1 oz feta cheese (drained weight),
    cut into 1-cm/½-inch cubes

Put the onion, aubergine, mushrooms and peppers on a large baking tray, placing the peppers cut side down. Oil lightly.

Grill for 10–12 minutes, turning the onion, aubergine and mushroom halfway through, until beginning to blacken. Cut into even-sized chunks. Place in a shallow ovenproof dish. Arrange the diced tomatoes on top. Season with salt and pepper.

Preheat the oven to 220°C/425°F/Gas Mark 7.

In a bowl, combine the garlic, parsley, rosemary, thyme and lemon peel with the breadcrumbs. Season with pepper. Add the 3 tablespoons of olive oil to bind the mixture together. Scatter the mixture over the vegetables. Add the olives and feta cheese.

Bake in the preheated oven for 10–15 minutes, or until the vegetables are heated through and the topping is crisp. Serve straight from the dish.

spinach, mushroom & rice gratin

easy serves 4

35 minutes 50 minutes

ingredients

1 tbsp olive oil

1 tbsp butter

1 onion, chopped finely

225 g/8 oz mushrooms, sliced finely

2 garlic cloves, chopped very finely

½ tsp dried thyme or oregano

¼ tsp dried chilli flakes

finely grated zest of ½ lemon

salt, to taste

450 g/1 lb spinach, stalks removed, leaves sliced into thin ribbons

200 g/7 oz long-grain rice

400 ml/14 fl oz water

¼–½ tsp pepper

115g/4 oz Edam or mild Cheddar cheese, coarsely grated

Heat the oil and butter in a large saucepan over a medium heat. Add the onion and mushrooms. Cook for 5 minutes, or until soft. Add the garlic, thyme, chilli flakes, lemon peel and salt to taste. Cook for a few seconds.

Add the spinach and stir until wilted. Stir in the rice and cook for a few minutes, or until the grains are translucent. Add the water and bring to the boil. Cover tightly and simmer over a low heat for 15–20 minutes, or until the water has been absorbed.

Preheat the oven to 180°C/350°F/Gas Mark 4.

Transfer the mixture to a lightly greased ovenproof baking dish. Season with the pepper. Sprinkle the cheese over the surface. Gently fork it into the rice.

Cover with foil. Bake in the preheated oven for about 20 minutes, until the cheese has melted.

Remove the foil and bake for 5 minutes more before serving.

aubergine gratin

very easy

serves 4
as a starter

15 minutes   40 minutes

ingredients

4 tbsp olive oil

2 onions, chopped finely

2 garlic cloves, chopped very finely

2 aubergines, sliced thickly

3 tbsp chopped fresh flat-leaved parsley

½ tsp dried thyme

salt and pepper

400 g/14 oz canned chopped tomatoes

175 g/6 oz mozzarella cheese, coarsely
  grated

6 tbsp freshly grated Parmesan cheese

Heat the oil in a frying pan over a medium heat. Add the onion and cook for 5 minutes, or until soft. Add the garlic and cook for a few seconds, or until just beginning to colour. Using a perforated spoon, transfer the onion mixture to a plate.

Cook the aubergine slices in batches in the same pan until they are just lightly browned.

Preheat the oven to 200°C/400°F/Gas Mark 6.

Arrange a layer of aubergine slices in the base of a shallow ovenproof dish. Sprinkle with some of the parsley, thyme, salt and pepper. Add layers of onion, tomatoes and mozzarella, sprinkling parsley, thyme, salt and pepper over each layer.

Continue layering, finishing with a layer of aubergine slices. Sprinkle with the Parmesan. Bake, uncovered, in the preheated oven for 20–30 minutes, or until the top is golden and the aubergines are tender. Serve hot.

Easy to prepare and quick to cook, fish and seafood make mouthwatering one-pot meals. Fresh or frozen, bottled or canned, a variety of fish and seafood can go into the pot. Firm-fleshed white fish, such as cod or snapper, are ideal since they maintain texture and succulence while gently simmering in a sauce. Plump, juicy prawns, briny clams, scallops and mussels also provide a taste of the ocean. The recipes include a Brazilian seafood stew, redolent with saffron, as well as rich, creamy chowders and a Cajun-style gumbo.

fish one-pots

seafood chowder

very easy   serves 4

40 minutes   40 minutes

ingredients

1 tsp vegetable oil

4 rashers streaky bacon

4 tbsp butter

1 large onion, chopped finely

2 celery sticks, quartered lengthways
   and diced

3 floury potatoes, cubed

3 tbsp chopped fresh parsley

1 tsp chopped fresh thyme

1 fresh bay leaf

salt and pepper

1.2 litres/2 pints hot milk

350 g/12 oz firm white fish, such as cod,
   haddock or hake, cut into chunks

280 g/10 oz clams (in jar)

6–8 peeled tiger prawns, halved

6 large scallops (optional), sliced thickly

Heat the oil in a frying pan over a medium–high heat. Cook the bacon until crisp. Drain on kitchen paper, crumble into bite-sized pieces and set aside.

Heat the butter in a large saucepan. Add the onion, celery and potatoes. Reduce the heat to medium–low. Cover and cook for 10 minutes, stirring occasionally, until beginning to soften.

Add 2 tablespoons of the parsley, the thyme and bay leaf. Season generously with salt and pepper. Pour in the hot milk. Cover and simmer for 15 minutes. Add the fish and continue cooking for 5 minutes.

Add the clams and their juice, the prawns, and scallops if using. Simmer for 5 minutes more.

Ladle into individual bowls. Serve garnished with the bacon pieces and the remaining parsley.

caribbean fish chowder

very easy   serves 4

35 minutes   45 minutes

ingredients

3 tbsp vegetable oil

1 tsp cumin seeds, crushed

1 tsp dried thyme or oregano

1 white onion, diced

½ green pepper, deseeded and diced

1 sweet potato, diced

2 or 3 green chillies, deseeded and very
finely chopped

1 garlic clove, chopped very finely

1 litre/1¾ pints chicken stock

salt and pepper

400 g/14 oz red snapper fillets, cut into
chunks

25 g/1 oz frozen peas

25 g/1 oz frozen sweetcorn kernels

125 ml/4 fl oz single cream

3 tbsp chopped fresh coriander

Heat the oil with the cumin seeds and thyme in a large saucepan over a medium heat. Add the onion, pepper, sweet potato, chillies and garlic. Cook, stirring, for 1 minute.

Reduce the heat to medium–low. Cover and cook for 10 minutes, or until beginning to soften.

Pour in the chicken stock. Season generously with salt and pepper. Bring to the boil, then cover and simmer over a medium–low heat for 20 minutes.

Add the red snapper, peas, sweetcorn and cream. Cook, uncovered, for 7–10 minutes, or until the fish is cooked.

Stir in the coriander just before serving.

prawn gumbo

very easy   serves 4

40 minutes   45 minutes

ingredients

2 tbsp vegetable oil

2 tbsp butter

250 g/9 oz okra, trimmed and sliced thickly

1 white onion, chopped finely

2 celery sticks, quartered lengthways and
  diced

1 green pepper, deseeded and diced

2 garlic cloves, chopped very finely

200 g/7 oz canned chopped tomatoes

½ tsp dried thyme or oregano

1 fresh bay leaf

salt and pepper

850 ml/1½ pints chicken stock or water

450 g/1 lb fresh or frozen raw prawns,
  shelled

few drops of Tabasco sauce

2 tbsp chopped fresh coriander

Heat the oil and butter in a large saucepan over a medium heat. Add the okra and cook, uncovered, for 15 minutes, or until it loses its gummy consistency.

Add the onion, celery, pepper, garlic, tomatoes, thyme and bay leaf. Season with salt and pepper. Cover and cook over a medium–low heat for 10 minutes.

Pour in the stock. Bring to the boil, then cover and simmer over a medium–low heat for 15 minutes, or until the vegetables are al dente. Add the prawns and Tabasco sauce. Cook for about 5 minutes, or until the prawns are pink.

Stir in the coriander just before serving.

brazilian seafood stew

easy   serves 4

30 minutes   35 minutes

ingredients

450 g/1 lb mussels, scrubbed
2 tbsp olive oil
1 onion, chopped finely
2 garlic cloves, chopped very finely
400 g/14 oz canned chopped tomatoes
¼ tsp cayenne
pinch of saffron threads

salt and pepper
900 g/2 lb cod steaks, cut into chunks
225 g/8 oz raw tiger prawns, peeled
200 g/7 oz canned crab meat
200 g/7 oz clams (in jar)
3 tbsp chopped fresh coriander

Remove the 'beards' from the mussels. Rinse the mussels well, to remove any sand, and discard any with broken shells or that remain open when tapped.

Heat the oil in a large saucepan or flameproof casserole over a medium heat. Add the onion and cook for 5 minutes, or until soft.

Stir in the garlic, tomatoes, cayenne and saffron. Season with salt and pepper. Cook for 5 minutes, stirring occasionally.

Add the cod and the cleaned mussels. Pour in enough water to just cover and bring to the boil. Reduce the heat to low. Cover and simmer for 10 minutes, or until the mussels open. Discard any that have not opened.

Add the prawns, crab meat and clams with their juice. Simmer for 5 minutes more, or until the prawns are pink.

Stir in the coriander just before serving.

chunky cod stew with celery & peppers

easy   serves 4

35 minutes   1 hour
            10 minutes

ingredients

2 red peppers, halved, cored and deseeded
3 tbsp olive oil
1 onion, chopped finely
2 garlic cloves, chopped very finely
1 tbsp white wine vinegar
1 tbsp tomato purée
1 tbsp dried thyme or oregano
250 ml/9 fl oz fish stock

salt and pepper
2 celery sticks, sliced finely
600 g/1 lb 5 oz fresh or frozen thick cod
    steaks, cut into chunks
55 g/2 oz stale, coarse breadcrumbs
8–10 black olives, stoned and sliced

chopped celery leaves, to garnish

Place the peppers cut side down on a baking tray under a preheated hot grill for 10–12 minutes until beginning to blacken. Heat 1 tablespoon of the olive oil in a shallow casserole. Cook the onion for 5 minutes, stirring. Add the garlic, vinegar, tomato purée and half the thyme or oregano. Cook, stirring, for 1 minute. Add the stock. Simmer for 5 minutes.

Preheat the oven to 200°C/400°F/Gas Mark 6. Remove the skin from the peppers. Roughly chop the flesh. Put in a blender or food processor with the onion mixture. Season with salt and pepper. Purée until smooth and pour into the casserole. Add the celery and cod. Bring to the boil, then cover and bake in the preheated oven for 35 minutes.

Combine the breadcrumbs, remaining oil, olives, remaining thyme, salt and pepper in a small bowl. Sprinkle over the fish. Brown under a hot grill for 5 minutes. Garnish with chopped celery leaves before serving.